A PORTRAIT OF
CHESTER

Rob Meighen

HALSGROVE

First published in Great Britain in 2006

British Library Cataloguing-in-Publication Data
A CIP record for this title is available from the British Library

ISBN 1 84114 492 4
ISBN 978 1 84114 492 4

HALSGROVE
Halsgrove House
Lower Moor Way
Tiverton, Devon EX16 6SS
Tel: 01884 243242
Fax: 01884 243325
email: sales@halsgrove.com
website: www.halsgrove.com

Printed and bound by D'Auria Industrie Grafiche Spa, Italy

DEDICATION

For Bella and our beautiful boy Finn.

Introduction

Chester is unique in having so much of its history on display. No longer contained by its ancient walls, it has grown into a bustling, cosmopolitan city while still managing to retain its ancient charm.

The walls are the longest and most complete city walls in the country, and today they form a pleasant promenade from which to enjoy a 2-mile stroll around the city. The layout of the main streets is still based on the original Roman grid-iron design of two thousand years ago. The name of the Roman fortress *Deva* came from the Celtic name for the goddess of the River Dee. *Dyfrdwy*, the Welsh name for the Dee, means water of the goddess.

The Roman amphitheatre is the largest stone-built amphitheatre of its type yet discovered in Britain. The long military history of Chester starts with the Romans, and Chester went on to become an important Saxon town, before William the Conqueror built the first castle here shortly after the Conquest.

Chester has outstanding black and white half-timbered buildings, and the medieval Rows retain their unique character to give the city some of the oldest shop frontages in the world. It was still a major military stronghold by the time of the Civil War in the seventeenth century. King Charles I is famously alleged to have stood on the tower on the city walls which takes his name to witness the defeat of his Royalist forces by the Parliamentarian New Model Army on the battlefield of Rowton Moor on 24 September, 1645.

Situated on the estuary of the River Dee, Chester has also always had a strong commercial life. It had a major network of medieval guilds with many skilled tradesmen, and for a long period of time Chester was one of the most important seaports in the country.

Chester remains one of Britain's most beautiful cities; unique in that it retains its sense of historical identity while emerging as a dynamic and modern centre. As a photographer I have been spoilt for choice as to where I could point my camera to find beautiful scenes. I hope to have done some justice to this magnificent city with which I have become so well acquainted. I have found Chester to be a place where the deeper you delve, the greater your reward.

The 144 images contained in this book were taken in a relatively short time during the spring, summer and autumn of 2005. I hope that this snapshot in time goes some way towards recording some of the two thousand years of history contained within the walls of this historic yet vibrant and forward-looking city.

Rob Meighen

The Old Dee Bridge

A bridge has stood on this site since Roman times, as it was of great strategic importance as the only way into North Wales from across the Dee. Handbridge, the suburb on the south side of the bridge (left) was burnt down so many times by the Welsh in the Middle Ages that they called it *Treboeth* – Welsh for 'burnt town'.

Opposite: **The Old Dee Bridge**

Comprising seven unequal arches and built much as we see it today in the late 1380s, the bridge is on the site of a succession of earlier wooden bridges and a pre-Roman fording place.

The Old Dee Bridge
Toll fees were abolished in 1885 after enough money had been raised to pay back the loan taken out for the construction of the Grosvenor Bridge. It cost 9d (4p) for a carriage and 2d (1p) for a saddled horse to cross the bridge.

The Old Dee Bridge

Ferryboats landed at the Shipgate, located at the foot of the castle. It was cheaper to cross the river that way than to pay the tolls on the nearby Old Dee Bridge. Some farmers even opted to wait until low tide and waded across the river with their animals to avoid paying altogether. Up until 1833, when the Grosvenor Bridge was completed, the Old Dee Bridge was the only way for traffic to enter Chester from across the river.

Sunset on a spring day
Behind the Old Dee Bridge stands County
Hall, headquarters of Cheshire County
Council. The Queen opened the Georgian-
style building in 1957, almost twenty years after
construction had commenced. It stands on
part of the site of old gaol of Chester Castle,
unfavourably compared by prison reformer
John Howard to the Black Hole of Calcutta.

The Old Dee Bridge

The River Dee, Weir and the Bridgegate
The total catchment area of the River Dee up to Chester Weir is approximately 1800 square kilometres (about 700 square miles).

The Weir
The Weir was built by the first Earl of Chester, Hugh d'Avranches, in 1092 to provide power for his corn mill by the Dee Bridge. For centuries the Earls of Chester and the Crown owned the Dee Mills. At their height in the seventeenth century, 11 water wheels were in operation and they provided a huge income, as all Cestrians were obliged to have their corn ground there.

The Groves

Chester's riverside promenade is popular with residents and visitors alike. It was laid out in two stages. Charles Croughton constructed the section below the city walls in 1725, and in 1880 the area nearest to the Old Dee Bridge was by built Alderman Charles Brown.

Opposite: **The Groves**

The Edwardian bandstand at The Groves was built at a cost of £350. The first band to play there was the Mounted Band of the Royal Artillery on 17 May, 1913.

Pleasure Boats at The Groves
For over a century, the public have been able to hire rowing boats or board a motor launch for a cruise
up river and a glimpse of Eaton Hall, seat of the Duke of Westminster.

Opposite: **The River Dee**
In Roman times, the Dee was an important shipping river, and in the thirteenth century,
Chester was the second most important port in Britain. Today Chester is no longer
a port and the river serves the people of Chester for a different purpose.

The Bank of Scotland
Situated on Queen's Park Road, the Bank of Scotland has a commanding
view across the Dee to The Groves.

The Groves
Pleasure boats depart from The Groves for cruises up the Dee.

Bridgegate
The present Bridgegate dates from 1782, when the medieval gate was demolished and replaced
with a Joseph Turner design, funded by the Corporation of the City of Chester.

Opposite: **Bridgegate**
The gate guarding the fourteenth-century Old Dee Bridge was of strategic importance because it guarded the only crossing place
on the Dee and was thus the only way into North Wales. Consequently it was heavily fortified with towers and gatehouses.

The city walls
Local artists sell and exhibit their work in a unique venue.

The Recorder's Steps
A couple browse the artwork for sale at the foot of the
Recorder's Steps, named after Roger Comberbach who
served as Recorder of Chester from 1700 to 1720.

Queen's Park Bridge
The present bridge replaced an earlier one built in 1852 by Enoch Gerrard which linked the newly-built suburb of Queen's Park to the town centre. Queen's Park was a villa estate laid out in the mid nineteenth century by Gerrard, who bought the land when it was advertised for sale in 1851.

Queen's Park Bridge at night
The bridge was opened on 18 April, 1923 in a ceremony conducted by the Mayor of Chester, Councillor S.R. Wall.

Reflection on the Dee
A reflection of Queen's Park Bridge captured in the River Dee. The bridge underwent major restoration in 1998.

Queen's Park Bridge
The contractors David Rowell & Co. completed this graceful iron bridge in 1923. It spans 275ft/84m over the River Dee.

The Riverside
The south bank opposite The Groves is another popular promenade.

Minerva shrine
Across the Old Dee Bridge on the south bank of the river lies the site of a huge Roman quarry which provided
the sandstone used for much of the Roman buildings of Chester, such as the amphitheatre, city walls
and bathhouse. Carved into an outcrop of sandstone is a shrine to the Roman goddess Minerva.

Minerva shrine
The shrine was much eroded over the two thousand years since it was carved, and it is now quite difficult to make out the figure of Minerva, who stood in a simplified temple. Minerva was the Roman goddess of war, knowledge and craftsmanship, and so would have been important to the soldiers working the quarry.

The riverside
Couples enjoy an autumnal day
on the banks of the river.

Cathedral gardens
The popular Cheshire Regiment Memorial Garden is set in the cathedral grounds.

Opposite: **Chester Cathedral**
Chester Cathedral is the most complete medieval monastic complex still standing
in Britain. With records of a church on this site since the early tenth century, it
was founded as a Benedictine monastery dedicated to St Werburgh on 1092. In 1541,
following the Dissolution of the Monasteries, it was rededicated as the
Cathedral Church of Christ and the Blessed Virgin Mary.

The Creation Window

Located in the thirteenth-century dining hall is the beautiful Creation Window. The artist Rosalind Grimshaw explained: 'I have taken the Creation story very literally; each of the upper lights representing one of the six days in which God created the world. The lower panels portray the continuation, development and possible future of the subjects and images in the upper lights. Above and overarching the four centre lights is the dove – the Holy Spirit – and reaching over the whole work is the Hand of God – creating and blessing.'

Opposite: **The interior of the cathedral**

Detail of the exterior of the cathedral
The cathedral was very heavily restored, most
notably by George Gilbert Scott who between
1868 and 1876 replaced much of the weathered
stonework, embellished the exterior with
battlements and pinnacles, and aroused much
criticism for destroying significant parts
of the medieval fabric.

The cathedral at dusk

The work of Sir George Gilbert Scott is clearly visible in this image of the cathedral tower with its battlements and pinnacles. In the late 1960s, the great tower was deemed no longer strong enough to house the cathedrals bells. They are now housed in the Addelshaw Tower, a purpose-built bell tower set in the cathedral grounds.

Abbey Square
This elegant square was built in the mid-eighteenth century on the site of the abbey bakery and brewery. The column in the central oval-shaped garden came from the old exchange building, and was erected here in 1756.

Detail of Abbey Square
Despite the terraced appearance of the buildings, they were individually constructed over a period of seventy years by several different developers. Most of the houses in the square are now used as offices.

2-18 St Werburgh Street
Chester architect John Douglas (1829-1911) developed the east side of Werburgh Street between 1895 and 1899.
He bought the land following Chester Corporation's decision to demolish the existing row of shops
in order to widen the approach to the cathedral.

Opposite: **St Werburgh Street**
As the developer and architect John Douglas planned to ensure the ordered development of the area, he designed
a Gothic row that was to be built in stone and brick. The Duke of Westminster made a special request to Douglas
that the half-timbered style be adopted in his designs. The resulting building is one of the finest examples of the
black-and-white revival, and one of Douglas's most celebrated works.

The Eastgate
Both the current and medieval
East Gates were built on the site of the
original East Gate of the Roman fortress.
The present Eastgate was built by
Mr Hayden at the expense of Richard,
Lord Grosvenor, in 1768-9.

Opposite: **The Northgate Clock**
The flags on the right of this image
are mounted on the Grosvenor Hotel,
built between 1863 and 1886 on the site
of the Royal Hotel. It was named in
honour of its owner Richard Grosvenor,
second Marquess of Westminster. On the
left is the Midland Bank, a grand red-
brick building designed by John Douglas
in a Dutch or Flemish style.

The Eastgate Clock

The famous Eastgate clock was added in 1899 to commemorate Queen Victoria's Diamond Jubilee which was in 1897, the date the clock bears on its face. John Douglas, the architect responsible for many of Chester's black-and-white buildings, designed the open wrought iron structure. His initial stone design was rejected on the grounds that it would block the light of neighbouring buildings.

Opposite: **The Eastgate**

The Eastgate was considered the main entrance to the city, and as such in the medieval period was the most elaborate of Chester's gates. From the late eighteenth century onwards, bridges replaced all four of Chester's main medieval gates. The wider span enabled promenading on the walls to continue while the increasing volume of traffic flowed below. The Eastgate was completed in 1769.

Street Performer

A musician entertains the crowds of Saturday shoppers on Eastgate Street. In the background standing between two fine examples of Chester's black-and-white half-timbered buildings is George William's stone-built Chester Bank.

Opposite: **Eastgate Street**

Chester's main shopping street contains some of its finest architecture, including the classical stone building which is presently home to the NatWest bank. It was designed by George Williams in 1860, and originally built as the headquarters of the Chester Bank.

Browns of Chester
This early Gothic building is known as the Crypt Building and is a fine example of T. M. Penson's *oeuvre*. It was built in 1858 and along with an earlier neighbouring building of 1828 forms the front of Browns of Chester.

Interior, Browns of Chester
Browns was once known as the 'Harrods of the North'. The family-run department store
was founded by Susannah Brown in the late eighteenth century and it is now owned
by the Debenhams group. The Brown family donated the park known as the
Earl's Eye to the people of Chester.

City commerce
Chester was recently ranked best city to visit and tenth most profitable in a survey of English towns
and cities. The six million visitors who visit Chester each year spend at least £320 million in
local shops, hotels, restaurants and attractions.

The High Cross

The High Cross had stood on this site since 1407 until it was destroyed during the fierce fighting of the
English Civil Wars 1642–1651. Today's cross was re-erected in 1975 and incorporates just two parts
of the original, which had remained hidden on the site of the Roman gardens until 1806.

The Cross Buildings
Designed by T. M. Lockwood, this fine block of black-and-white Victorian mock-
Tudor buildings was commissioned by the first Duke of Westminster.

The High Cross
The High Cross was for centuries the heart of the city; the Mayor, Aldermen and the City Council came to meet here, as did merchants and their customers. The cross would have originally been gilded, brightly-painted and covered in religious imagery.

Opposite: **The Rows**
New bridges have been built over side streets in order to provide continuous pedestrian routes and retain the character of The Rows. The City Council is now responsible for The Rows, and it ensures that any new development in the area incorporate them into the design.

The Rows, Bridge Street
Standing on Bridge Street is this former art gallery, built in the ninteenth century. A statue of King Charles I with orb and sceptre is the centrepiece of the art gallery front, which is also decorated with biblical scenes.

The Rows

Chester's unique shopping galleries or 'rows' date from the Middle Ages. By the mid fourteenth century there was an extensive network containing more rows than survive today. The Rows existence is owed to a combination of factors. The city developed along the Roman gridiron pattern of streets and was contained by the defensive walls, leaving little land for building. The street level is much the same as it was in Roman times but the land behind the main street is often a storey higher. Roman ruins survived until the thirteenth century, and as they slowly collapsed, debris built up thus raising the level.

The Three Old Arches

The Three Old Arches form the façade of a building dating from 1274, so it is perhaps the oldest shop frontage to survive in England. In the fourteenth century, the rear of the building was rebuilt and enlarged to include an impressive stone-walled hall.

St Michael's Church
The Chester Heritage Centre
currently occupies St Michael's Church.
A dwindling congregation led the church
to be declared redundant in 1972.
The Chester Heritage Centre was Britain's
first architectural heritage centre
when it was opened in 1975.

St Michael's Church

St Michael's Church dates from 1150, although it has gone through a number of major restorations.
The most notable of these was a Victorian remodelling between 1849 and 1851, when the church
was almost completely rebuilt to the designs of the Chester architect James Harrison.

St Michael's Row and Arcade

The most impressive building on Bridge Street is the massive entrance to St Michael's Arcade. This was built in 1910 in the baroque style and faced with white and gold Royal Doulton tiles. There was very strong public opposition to the building's appearance, and following petitions from the City Council and the Bishop the owner, the second Duke of Westminster agreed to demolish the façade.

St Michael's Row and Arcade
The façade was demolished and then re-erected in the familiar black-and-white revival style. The estimated cost to the Duke was £4000 in 1911, roughly £2.1 million today, a costly misjudgement of the Cestrian's strength of feeling towards their favoured black-and-white architecture.

Jones's Wine Bar
Jones's Wine Bar is located in one of Chester's signature black-and-white mock-Tudor buildings.

Opposite: **Chester Town Hall**
William Henry Lynn of Belfast designed the grey and red sandstone building. Its central diagonally-set tower is 160 ft (49m) high and dominates the square beneath. For over a hundred years the tower was without a clock, and was only altered in 1987 when three clock faces were added. The side facing the Welsh hills was left empty, and the joke is that Chester won't give the Welsh the time of day.

A Celebration of Chester
This bronze sculpture by Stephen Broadbent entitled A Celebration of Chester was created as part of the cathedral's 900th anniversary celebrations in 1992. The intertwining figures symbolise protection, industry and thanksgiving. In the foreground a preacher tries his best to spread God's word to Saturday shoppers.

Opposite: **Chester Town Hall**
The Prince of Wales, later King Edward VII, opened Chester's Gothic Town Hall on 15 October, 1869. It was built to replace the seventeenth-century (1698) Exchange, which formerly stood in the middle of the square but was destroyed by fire in 1862.

Chester Town Hall
Along with the cathedral,
the Town Hall dominates
the city's skyline.

City tour bus
One of the best ways to appreciate Chester's
two thousand years of history is to take one of
the guided open-top sightseeing bus tours.

Walking the walls
The city can be circumnavigated by using the
walls. The complete circuit is approximately
2 miles and is enduringly popular with
Cestrians and visitors alike.

Water Tower gardens and maze

In medieval times, the Dee flowed up to the city walls and would have covered the park and maze on the site today. The curved maze pathways symbolize the natural flow of water and the circular character of the maze reflects the shape of the ancient tower.

The Water Tower

The round red sandstone tower was built to protect the town from being attacked through its busy commercial port. Construction of the Water Tower and a spur wall to connect it to the existing walls was begun in 1322 and completed in 1326. Now that the River Dee has changed its course, the tower stands in beautiful public gardens.

The canal, railway and walls

In 1846, the medieval wall was breached here in two places for the construction of the Chester to Holyhead railway line.
The two pedestrian bridges were built to retain the public right of way on the walls and to permit access to
Bonewaldesthorne's Tower, seen through the trees on the right. In 1838 a *camera obscura* was installed
in the tower; it is still there and in working order, although the tower is rarely opened to the public.

Bonewaldesthorne's Tower

The unusually-named Bonewaldesthorne's Tower was constructed to protect the exposed corner of the city walls, and guarded the entrance to the port in the river below. Over time, the course of the river has changed, and seven hundred years ago, the New Tower, now known as the Water Tower, was built at the river's edge. Since then the waters have continued receding and both towers are now some distance from the Dee.

The Queen's School
The first students enrolled at The Queen's School in 1878, when it was known as Chester School for Girls.
The name was changed when Queen Victoria issued a royal decree commanding that the school should
'henceforth be known as "The Queen's School."' The Queen's School remains the only school
in the country granted the privilege of bearing this name.

Overleaf: **Southbound across the river**
A train leaving Chester crosses the Dee railway bridge on its way south. The first railways came
to Chester in 1840, when lines opened to Birkenhead and Crewe.

The Roodee
As well as horse racing, kite flying is also popular on the open area known as the Roodee.

Warming up for the race

The founding father of racing at the Roodee was Henry Gee. Mayor of Chester in 1540, he cancelled the traditional Shrove Tuesday ball game between the Shoemakers and the Drapers Companies because of its increasingly violent nature and replaced it with racing. His other legacy is that his name is still used in 'the Gee Gees' – used to describe horse racing.

The Roodee
The river once flowed right up to the walls, where today thousands stand to cheer on the winners.
From May to September, 12 meetings take place at the Roodee of which the Chester Cup is the most
renowned. At this meeting in 2004, over 10,000 bottles of champagne were consumed.

Opposite: **Chester Racecourse**
The Roodee is the home to the oldest racecourse in Britain. The 65-acre site derives its name
from the Saxon *rood* – meaning a cross, and the Norse suffix *eye* – meaning an island, so it is literally
'the island of the cross.' In Saxon times the entire site was submerged under water with the exception
of a small island in the middle on which a stone cross stood. It is still possible to see the
stump of this in the middle of the course.

The Watergate
When Chester was a flourishing port in the Middle Ages, the river flowed close to the Watergate. All goods entering the city from the port passed through this gate. After the canalisation of the Dee in the 1730s, a new port was built lower down the river.
The present arch, designed by Joseph Turner, replaced the medieval Watergate in 1788.

The Northgate

The Northgate is a classical arch designed by Thomas Harrison and built in 1807–10.
Commissioned by Earl Grosvenor when he was Mayor in 1807-08, he objected to the
original design, which was similar to the Watergate. The City Council accepted his
objections when he offered to erect the gate at his own expense.

Fountains Roundabout

The roundabout, just beyond the Northgate, was built in the 1960s as part of the city's Inner Ring Road scheme. The architectural historian Sir Nikolaus Pevsner (1902-83) rather disparagingly commented: 'The roundabout with the well-intentioned fountain destroys the street continuity, and indeed the town scale.'

Opposite: **The Town Crier and the Railway Station**

The station clock was moved into this off-centre location after the construction of the Queen Hotel in 1860-61 had blocked the view of it to travellers approaching the station along City Road.

The Town Crier
Located on the corner of City Road and Station Road, the Town Crier was originally opened as the Queen Commercial Hotel and was linked to the Queen Hotel on the opposite corner via an underground passageway.

The Queen Hotel
The Queen Hotel is located directly across from Chester Railway Station. It was opened on 21 April, 1860 and cost £29,000.
T. M. Penson designed it in an Italianate style. Pevsner described it as: 'four-storied and Italianate, with a big porch,
the whole composition stodgy as these Italianate hotels tend to be'.

Telford's Warehouse

The renowned Georgian engineer Thomas Telford (1757-1854) was responsible for the design and construction of this canal-side building. It stands partly on land and partly on water. The reason for this was to allow canal boats to be loaded or unloaded from the full height of the loading bay within the building. In the 1980s, the building was converted into a public house and restaurant retaining much of its character and sense of history. It also has a fine reputation as a live music venue.

Lock gate

Originally five locks were built to take the Chester Canal on its final descent to the River Dee.
When the canal was linked with the Ellesmere Canal in the 1790s, the bottom two locks were filled in.
It is still possible to navigate to the Dee through a graving dock then through this lock gate.

Mill Hotel

The 129-bedroom Mill Hotel stands on a site which straddles the Shropshire Union Canal. Moored outside the bar area is a 70ft (21m) restaurant boat, which offers dining cruises along the Union Canal.

The Bridge of Sighs

The small bridge at the top of this image was built in 1793. It once connected the City Gaol to the Chapel of St John in the south wing of the Blue Coat School. Prisoners taken there from the gaol to receive the last rites would have given a last sigh as they crossed back to the gaol to meet their deaths – hence the name.

Shropshire Canal and deep cutting
Begun in 1772, the Chester Canal was intended
to attract trade from Liverpool and the Midlands
by linking the Port of Chester with the new Trent
and Mersey Canal. It was a financial failure.
When completed in 1779, the canal only reached
Nantwich, 19 miles away. In 1795 the Wirral
branch of the Ellesmere Canal opened, connecting
Chester to the River Mersey at Ellesmere Port.
Packet boats provided a busy passenger service
between Liverpool and Tower Wharf.

A Roman cutting?
This deep cutting carrying the Chester Canal is reputed to date from Roman times. The exact size and depth of the original defensive ditch is uncertain. Over the centuries people discarded rubbish from the city walls gradually filling it in. It was a welcome discovery for the contractors digging the canal in the 1770s, who had originally thought they would have to dig the full depth through solid sandstone.

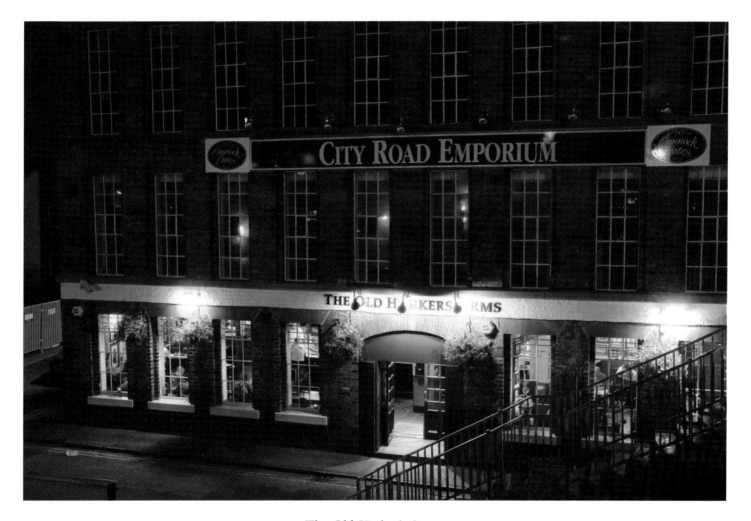

The Old Harker's Arms
The name of this popular canal-side pub is taken from a Mr Harker who was the proprietor of a canal-boat chandlers once located there. Harkers, as it is known locally, is a regular in the *Good Pub Guide*.

Shropshire Canal and Steam Mill
The Steam Mill in the background of this photograph is a Grade II listed building dating from 1834, although it was
rebuilt after a fire in 1864. It has been converted into six floors of modern office accommodation,
complete with a large glass atrium and a restaurant and bar on the ground floor.

Albion Street

The well-maintained terraced houses seen here in Albion Street were erected between 1865 and 1869 on the former bowling green and pleasure gardens of the old Albion Hotel.

Albion Inn

Viewed here from the top of the walls, the Albion Inn is located on the corner of Park Street and Albion Street.
It is a fine example of a Victorian pub, and thanks to the incumbent landlord has retained much of its character
and traditional atmosphere. But note the rather unfriendly sign on the door: 'No Children, Family hostile'.

The Nine Houses
Built in 1655 the Nine Houses, of which only six survive, were restored by Chester City Council
in 1969. They are the only examples of pre-nineteenth century almshouses in Chester.

The Roman Gardens

The Roman Gardens stand on the site of a clay-tobacco-pipe factory, which was operational from at least 1781 until 1917. The gardens date from the 1950s, when a public park was created to display a collection of finely-carved building fragments from the Roman legionary fortress of *Deva*. The City Council extended the gardens in 2000 in order to provide another route down to the river.

Pepper Street Car Park
The lion placed on top of the car park was originally a prominent feature of the
Red Lion Brewery which previously occupied the site. It was rescued from
demolition and now adds character to the Chester skyline.

The amphitheatre walls and Newgate

Discovered by accident during building work in 1929, the amphitheatre has stood on this site since the late 70s AD. It was built originally as a timber-framed construction by the Roman Legion II *Adiutrix Pia Fidelis* (Supporting and Faithful) soon after the establishment of the *Deva* fortress. Legion XX *Valeria Victrix* (Strong and Victorious) rebuilt the amphitheatre in stone at the end of the first century. The Newgate is a relatively modern structure, designed by Sir Walter and Michael Tapper and opened in 1938.

Archaeology at the amphitheatre

The amphitheatre site is only partially excavated and is at present the subject of a major archaeological project. In a partnership between English Heritage and Chester City Council, a top team of experts are uncovering new results which are not only adding to the story of Chester but the worldwide knowledge of Roman history.

Opposite: **The legionaries' amphitheatre**

Some latter-day Romans continue the tradition of the Roman legionaries who used the amphitheatre as a practice ground for weapon training. A small altar dedicated to Nemesis, the Greek goddess of retribution and vengeance, was found near the north entrance. This gives us an insight into the more bloodthirsty events to which the arena might have played host. In its heyday, over 7000 spectators could have witnessed gladiatorial battles, animal fights and executions here.

The Church of St John the Baptist
This has been a site of Christian worship for nearly thirteen centuries, and the present church building has stood for over nine hundred years. At either end of it lay ruins; to the east the ruins of three chapels (seen here), and to the west a ruined tower. During the Civil War, Parliamentarian forces captured the church and raised a cannon with tackle to the top of the tower where it was used to bombard the town and breach the city walls in the Roman Gardens. Snipers were also positioned inside and Sheriff Ralph Richardson was killed by a shot from the tower.

Norman arch, St John's Church
Great mounds of soil and rubble were removed from St John's Church in 1871,
when the ruins were discovered as we see them today.

Norman arches, St John's Church
St John's church was shortened and the three east end chapels were left in ruins after the church lost its
collegiate status at the time of the Dissolution. This photograph shows a round-headed
Norman arch and a later Gothic pointed arch.

Opposite: **Coffin, St John's Church**
The coffin was discovered in the nineteenth century and set high into the ruins so that it could be seen
above the tall wall which once surrounded the graves. The coffin dates from the Middle Ages and
is carved from a single piece of oak. It is inscribed with the words 'Dust to Dust'.

Lumley Place

These pretty almshouses were built in 1872. Almshouses are charitable housing provided to enable elderly or poor people to continue to live in the community. They are often targeted at the poor, at those from certain forms of previous employment or their widows, and are generally maintained by a charity or the trustees of a bequest.

The Anchorite's Cell

This small sandstone building was built as a religious retreat for a reclusive monk. According to legend, King Harold was the reclusive monk living in the Anchorite's Cell. It is said that he wasn't killed at the Battle of Hastings in 1066 but merely blinded, and that he came to Chester to live as a hermit after the battle. Whatever the truth of the tale, the cell is now occupied, having been converted back into a dwelling in the nineteenth century.

St John's Vicarage
Built in the 1750s on Vicar's Lane opposite the Church of St John, the old vicarage remained in use as the vicarage until 1957. The Grosvenor Club then occupied it and currently it is used as offices.

The Lodge, Grosvenor Park

Richard, the second Marquess of Westminster gave the 20 acres that form Chester's famous Grosvenor Park to the city. On 9 October, 1867, he wrote to the City Council: 'I am desirous of placing the park on the hands of the corporation as a gift on my part to the citizens of Chester, hoping it may afford health and recreation to themselves and their families for many years to come.' John Douglas designed Grosvenor Park Lodge, shown here. Built in the 1860s in the black-and-white style, it is decorated with statues representing the Norman Earls of Chester.

Grosvenor Park miniature railway
The Marquess also paid for the design and laying out of the new pleasure park by the famous Edward Kemp,
landscape designer and former pupil of Joseph Paxton, the architect of Crystal Palace.
Here we see the miniature railway train taking a tour of the park.

Grosvenor Park
The whole of the park area was originally made up of fields. The official opening of Grosvenor Park was accompanied by the grandest ever procession witnessed in Chester, over a mile in length. A recent addition to the park is the Scented Garden for the Blind, which contains a specially-commissioned statue designed for visitors to feel.

Billy Hobbie's Well

This ancient well known as Billy Hobbie's Well
was enclosed with an ornate stone canopy
designed by John Douglas. It has a long tradition
as a wishing well but only apparently for girls,
as the following poem explains:

I lov'd the tales that idle maids would tell
Of wonders wrought at Billy Hobbie's Well;
Where love-sich girls with leg immured would stand,
The right leg t'was – the other on dry land,
With face so simple, stocking in the hand,
Wishing for husbands half a winter's day
With ninety times the zeal they used to pray.

Grosvenor Park Road

This row of houses was built by the famous Chester architect John Douglas in 1880. As developer and architect Douglas was able to create a group of buildings that are to this day regarded as some of his finest work. Sir Nikolaus Pevsner wrote of the buildings: 'How much more convincing Douglas is where the temptation to fussiness inherent in the magpie technique is avoided.'

Overleigh Water Tower
A local landmark, the Water Tower now has a secondary function
as it contains a mobile phone antenna.

Overleigh Cemetery

This peaceful Victorian cemetery was built to accommodate the city's dead when there was no longer any space in the city's church graveyards. Thomas Mainwaring Penson designed it and the first person buried here was Mr Ayrton of Abbots Grange in 1850. Penson was a well-known Chester architect who designed the Gothic part of Browns, the Queen Hotel and The Grosvenor Hotel. Thomas Lockwood and John Douglas are two more famous Chester architects buried here.

The Phoenix Tower

First known as Newton's Tower after the suburb it overlooks, and more famously King Charles' Tower because King Charles stood on the tower on 24 September, 1645 and witnessed his defeated army routed from the battlefield at Rowton Moor by the Parliamentarian New Model Army. The tower guards the northeast corner of Chester's walls and originally dates from the late thirteenth century. It was refurbished in 1613 by a two of the city's guilds, the Guild of Barber Surgeons and the Guild of Painters. The heraldic emblem of the Painters' Guild is a phoenix, which has given the tower its modern name.

Chester Castle
Within the medieval city walls lies Chester Castle. Originally built by William the Conqueror in 1070
to guard the Welsh border, it later became the Royal base for the military conquest of North Wales.

Chester Castle

Thomas Harrison's original commission to build a new gaol was extended to include the rebuilding of the original medieval Shire Hall. Work on this building ran for ten years until 1801, resulting in the building visible here through the entrance with its impressive colonnaded portico. The success of this project meant that permission was given to Harrison to further develop the castle, adding new barracks and an armoury block as east and west wings to the main body of the building. The castle now extends far beyond the medieval curtain wall.

Chester Castle
Pictured here rising above the walls is Napier House, built as the new armoury
between 1830–32 and designed by Captain Kitson.

Chester Castle
The grand entrance in the Greek Doric style was erected between 1810 and 1822, to complete the rebuilding of the castle complex of 1788-1822. The freestanding structure is based on the *Propylaeum* at the west end of the Acropolis in Athens. This was to be Harrison's final work on the castle.

St Mary's-on-the-Hill, seen through County Hall
St Mary's dates from 1350 and was built to serve the needs of the castle garrison. The graveyard was used to bury people who had been executed in the castle, including three alleged witches in the seventeenth century.

Opposite: **The Assize Court**
The Assize Court with its impressive
portico forms the centrepiece of Harrison's
design. Each of its 12 Doric columns
is formed from one single stone
23 feet (7m) in height.

Chester Castle
The statue of Queen Victoria bears the
following inscription: 'This statue was
erected in honour of a good and beloved
Queen and in grateful remembrance of her
long and glorious reign by her Majesty's
loyal subjects in the county and city
of Chester A.D. 1903.'

On statue plinth:
CAPE OF GOOD HOPE.
MALLAVELLY, SERINGAPATAM.
WEST INDIES.
BHURTPORE.

ERECTED
IN HONOR OF
STAPLETON COTTON
VISCOUNT COMBERMERE
FIELD MARSHAL

Stapleton Cotton
This statue commemorates the life of Stapleton
Cotton, first Viscount Combermere, who
fought in the French and Napoleonic Wars.
Baron Marochetti created it in the late 1860s.

Opposite: **Pastarazzi Ristorante**
James Harrison won a competition to design
the former Trustee Savings Bank building built
between 1851–3. The Grade II listed building
is now occupied by Pastarazzi Ristorante,
which opened in 1996.

The Grosvenor Museum
The Duke of Westminster laid the foundation stone for the museum in 1885, having donated the land on which it stands and giving £4000 towards its construction. The building is listed Grade II and the architect T. M. Lockwood designed this and many of Chester's Victorian black-and-white buildings.

The Grosvenor Museum
The museum contains many fine collections. The award-winning Roman Stones Gallery tells the story of the lives (and deaths) of the people of Roman Chester. The Art Gallery on the first floor contains an important collection of paintings, watercolours drawings and prints connected with Chester. The Ridgeway Silver Gallery, opened by the Prince of Wales in 1992, contains unique examples of Chester silver.

The Grosvenor Museum
The grand entrance to the museum.

A fierce welcome
A Roman soldier guards the reception area of the museum.

Tourist information sign
A tourist information sign helps one of Chester's six million yearly visitors navigate the attractions.
The city is home to 120,000 people, known as Cestrians.

Stanley Place

Built as a fine town house in 1591 for Sir Peter Warburton, a lawyer and MP for the city, it passed as his daughter's dowry to the Stanleys of Alderley. In 1866, it narrowly avoided being dismantled and transported to the USA and its future was only secured in 1889 when it was sold to the Derby Family on condition it would be preserved. The Earl of Derby gave Stanley Place to Chester City Corporation in 1928 and it is still owned by the City but managed by the Friends of Stanley Place.

Chester Business Park

Cheshire's largest office park has become home to major companies looking to set up their UK and European headquarters and call centres. It was established in 1985/86 with the arrival of Marks and Spencer Financial Services.

Opposite: **Chester Business Park**

Chester Business Park provides over one million square feet of office space for over 50 companies which employ approximately 7000 people.

The Bear & Billet
The Bear & Billet dates from 1664 and was built as a town house for the Earls of Shrewsbury who controlled
the nearby Bridgegate. When it became a pub over three hundred years ago, it took its name from
the bear shackled to a billet (stake) on the Earls of Shrewsbury's coat of arms.

Ye Olde Edgar

Dating from around 1570, this Grade I listed building was originally constructed as two town houses and was later converted into an inn called Ye Olde Edgar. The name was a tribute to King Edgar, who was rowed across the Dee by in 973 by eight British princes as a token of their submission to him. The building is now once again used as two dwellings.

View from the walls
The River Dee with The Groves
promenade alongside, viewed
from the city walls.

Boats on the River Dee
The River Dee is 70 miles (110 km) long. It rises in Snowdonia and discharges into the sea 12 miles west of Liverpool at Deeside.

Deva Terrace
As the sun burns away the last wisps of morning mist, a rower powers his way upstream on the Dee. In the background stands Deva Terrace, a stately Georgian construction of 17 three-storey houses. The houses are listed Grade II and have stunning views over the parkland of the Earl's Eye, also known as the Meadows.

The Meadows

Also known as the Earl's Eye, the Meadows is a huge and beautiful area of grass and wetlands bordering the river. It was presented to the city by the Mr and Mrs H. F. Brown (of Browns of Chester) in the late 1920s on the condition that it remained permanently open to the people of Chester 'as a public park, recreation ground, or lands for cricket, football or other games and recreations'.

Sunrise over the Meadows
Rowing on the Dee remains an ever-popular activity for Cestrians. The Chester
Regatta has been held on the River Dee since 1733, when most of the competitors
were men and women engaged in fishing, using their own boats and coracles
to race against each other in mixed doubles.

Opposite: **Grosvenor Bridge**
Grosvenor Bridge was, at the time of its construction, the largest single span stone arch
in Europe at 61m (200 feet) across and 18m (60 feet) high. It was designed by Thomas
Harrison and was his last work, as he died four years after its completion. William Cole
and the famous Liverpool dock engineer Jesse Hartley took over the project

The view from Grosvenor Bridge
There are a number of imposing mansions built on Curzon Park North that stand high on the south bank of the Dee.

Opposite: **Grosvenor Bridge at sunset**
The bridge was formally opened on 17 October, 1832, when the thirteen-year-old Princess Victoria (five years before she became Queen), accompanied by her mother, the Duchess of Kent, was driven through a triumphal arch decorated with the Royal arms erected in the centre of the still-unfinished bridge. A 21-gun salute was fired from the Castle Square and the Princess gave a short speech, in which she declared: 'I seize the occasion of our being the first persons to pass over this magnificent bridge to lend myself to the feeling that prevails, and to name it Grosvenor Bridge'. The bridge was completed and opened to traffic in November 1833.

Sunrise over St Mary-without-the-Walls
St Mary-without-the-Walls is located on the south bank of the river in Handbridge
and is viewed here at sunrise from the Grosvenor Bridge. The Duke and Duchess of
Westminster founded the parish church in 1885 and it was completed in 1887.